Please return / renew by date shown
You can renew it at:
norlink.norfolk.gov.uk
or by telephone: 0344 800 8006
Please have your librar

**A BOOT UP**

# THE
# NORFOLK COAST

## BOOK TWO
### Between Wolferton & Overstrand

Tony Rothe

First published in Great Britain in 2011

Front cover: *Overstrand Cliff*.  Back cover: *Blakeney Boats*

British Library Cataloguing-in-Publication Data
A CIP record for this title is available from the British Library

ISBN 978 0 85710 032 0

**PiXZ Books**
Halsgrove House, Ryelands Industrial Estate,
Bagley Road, Wellington, Somerset TA21 9PZ
Tel: 01823 653777
Fax: 01823 216796
email: sales@halsgrove.com

An imprint of Halstar Ltd, part of the Halsgrove group of companies
Information on all Halsgrove titles is available at: www.halsgrove.com

Printed and bound in China by Toppan Leefung Printing Ltd

## Contents

# Introduction

The Norfolk coastline must be one of the most varied in Great Britain, including as it does wild desolate fenlands, thriving docks and ports, towering cliffs, gently rolling countryside, isolated salt marshes, nationally famous bird reserves, shingle beaches, deserted sands, colourful heathlands, a steam railway, and charming seaside towns and villages – it's all here for the discerning tourist. You will find that the north-east section belies Norfolk's reputation for flatness – The last Ice Age just clipped the North Norfolk coast, and the glacier stopped a mile or two inland. Therefore this stretch of coast is built mainly of moraine, ie debris left by the melting glacier when the Ice Ages finished some 12 000 years ago, and has been continually moulded and shaped by the weather and sea ever since.

This second book covering the North Norfolk Coast contains 10 more walks covering the area from Terrington St Clement, not far from Wolferton, near King's Lynn, Norfolk's border with Lincolnshire, to Overstrand, just to the east of Cromer. There is something for everyone – Seaside, cliffs, fields, hills, marshes and heath, containing many wildlife habitats – walks that will appeal to every member of the family.

## How to use this book

This book is not aimed at serious long distance walkers. You won't necessarily need long woolly socks, plus-fours, heavy rucksacks, or even proper walking boots, although waterproof footwear is recommended for some of the walks, especially in winter, or in wet weather.

All the walks are circular, ie they bring you back to your starting point, and are between 0.8 and 3.3 miles long, although some of the longer walks have optional short-cuts. When walking casually you will be doing about 2 miles per hour, a more purposeful pace will get you along at about 3 miles an hour, so the shortest walks need take you no more than half an hour, whereas the longest can take you up to two hours.

And it's difficult to get lost — whenever you get a glimpse of the sea, well that's roughly to the north (except walk 1 when the distant sea is roughly west). If it's midday, then the sun is to the south (more to the east in the morning, more to the west in the evening, but never due north!). However, carrying a compass is always a good idea.

Sketch maps are included, but if you want a definitive map, then the Ordnance Survey Explorer maps (1:25000 series) are unbeatable. The first walk is on map 250 Norfolk Coast West, walks 2 to 7 are on map 251 Norfolk Coast Central, whereas the rest are on map 252 Norfolk Coast East.

Starting points are given, together with the British Grid reference which will enable you to find the spot on any Ordnance Survey map. Each starting point provides somewhere to park, but in some cases there may be a parking fee. A regular bus service, known as the "Coasthopper" (www.norfolkgreen.co.uk) runs along the coast linking many of the walks, and Sheringham is on "the Bittern" railway line. Nearest toilets and refreshments are suggested, but you must realise that many places are seasonal, so please don't complain if the ice cream man isn't where you expect to find him on a bitterly cold Tuesday morning in February!

The difficulty of each walk is indicated by a "boot" rating, based mainly on the quality of the paths, the gradients, and likely amount of mud! However, these are based on Norfolk standards: Compared to many walks in the Lake District or Pennines, the walks in this book would probably all rank as "1 boot". Most of these walks are not suitable for push-chairs, but this information is also given for each walk.

So, please use this little book to explore a very beautiful corner of a wonderful and varied part of the UK, and have fun doing so.

Tony Rothe, January 2011

# Key to Symbols Used

## Level of difficulty:

Easy 🐾

Fair 🐾 🐾

More challenging 🐾 🐾 🐾

## Map symbols:

🚗 Park & start

––––– Tarred Road

- - - - - Footpath

■ Building / Town

+ Church

🪣 Pub

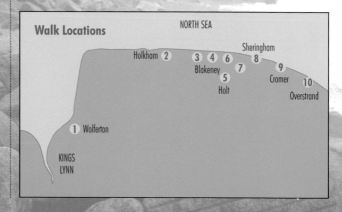

**Walk Locations**

NORTH SEA

Holkham ②

③ ④ ⑥

Blakeney

⑤

Holt

⑦

Sheringham

⑧

⑨

Cromer

⑩

Overstrand

① Wolferton

KINGS LYNN

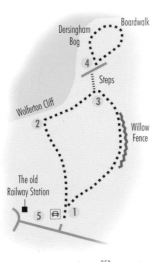

## 1 Wolferton

**Cliff and Nature Reserve:** *medieval clifftop walk and a royal train station*

This is the shortest walk in this book, and takes you along a short stretch of medieval clifftop, which once marked the line of the coast. A short diversion down a long flight of steps gives you the chance to walk around a tiny bit of Dersingham Bog, then it's back up the steps to return to your car. A further short stroll along the road west into the village would then take you to a beautifully preserved royal railway station, which is, unfortunately, no longer open to the public.

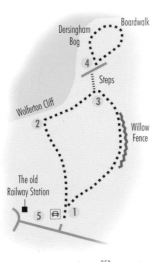

Boardwalk
Dersingham Bog
4
Steps
Wolferton Cliff
3
2
Willow Fence
The old Railway Station
5
1

| 250 m |

**Difficulty:** 🥾
Optional diversion: 🥾 🥾
**Start/Parking:** Small Car Park on northern side of northern approach road to the village, just to the east of the village (free)
**Map Ref:** TF 663284
Nearest postcode PE31 6HF
**Distance:** 0.5 miles (0.8 miles with optional diversion)
**Nearest toilets:** None
**Refreshments:** Sandringham Estate (2 miles)
**Terrain:** Good paths. One long flight of steps (on optional diversion)
**Transport:** Coasthopper bus
**Pushchairs:** Yes
Optional diversion: No

**1** Take the path at the back of the car park heading north ie away from the road. Go through the gate, and take the left hand path, signposted "Wolferton Cliff". Continue heading north to the clifftop, where an information board gives you information about the medieval cliff.

**2** Follow the path to the right and keep on the sandy path

*Longshore drift is responsible for the build up of land to the west of what was once a coastal cliff, lapped by waves, 1000 years ago. You can still see the sea over the treetops, but it is now a mile and a half away!*

*Path up Wolferton Cliff*

with views over heathland and pine trees. The valley below you would have carried the railway line north towards Hunstanton prior to 1966.

When you reach a bend to the right, you have the option of taking the path left, down a long flight of steps, then across the track on to a wooden boardwalk. This is Dersingham Nature Reserve, or Dersingham Bog, and is managed by English Nature. The reserve comprises three distinct habitats, mire, heath and woodland, attracting birds such as redpoll, cross-bill, long-eared owl, tree pipit and sparrowhawk.

 The short boardwalk gives you access to a small part of the reserve, and this diversion adds about 0.3 miles to this short walk. Return up the steps, resting at the seat at the top if you wish. The seat was dedicated to the singer John Denver in September 2006 by a group of local enthusiasts.

Turn left to continue your walk, and continue alongside a low willow fence back to the car park.

 If you have time for a further stroll, leave the car park turn right to head downhill for about 300 yards to view the old railway station. The railway line was opened in 1862 to link the royal family estate of Sandringham, bought by Queen Victoria as a coming-of-age present for

*Dersingham Bog - Boardwalk*

her eldest son Edward, directly through to London Kings Cross. Over the years the station at Wolferton was extended into a large suite of rooms providing luxurious and comfortable accommodation for visiting dignitaries to be entertained by the royal family whilst their luggage was transported up to the royal estate. The railway line was used extensively by successive royal families, and when King George VI died at Sandringham in 1952 the royal station and line were used to transport his body back to London. Unfortunately in 1966 the line and the station were closed. The station became a museum for a while, but is now a private residence not open to the public, although it can be seen externally from the road.

Wolferton Station

# 2 **Holkham**

***Park and Lake:*** *superb country estate, lakeside, and a fine church*

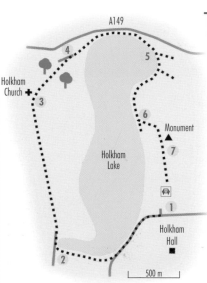

This is a straightforward walk around a little of the beautiful parkland surrounding the Palladian style Holkham Hall, built between 1734 and 1764 by Thomas Coke, Earl of Leicester. The Coke family still lives at the Hall and, with tenants, still farms the estate's 6100 hectares. Over the years the estate has diversified and now includes a holiday park at nearby Wells-next-the-Sea, a public house, two cafés, the Holkham Pottery, gift shops and more than 300 locally tenanted houses. Please make sure you

**Difficulty:**

**Start/Parking:** Main car park in front of Holkham Hall (currently free)

**Map Ref:** TF 885429

Nearest postcode NR23 1RS

**Distance:** 2.2 miles

**Nearest toilets:** Toilets in car park

**Refreshments:** Cafe & ice creams in courtyard beside Holkham Hall (when open)

**Terrain:** Grassy, woodland and lakeside paths

**Transport:** Coasthopper bus

**Pushchairs:** Yes

respect the estate, particularly by closing gates behind you.

*Holkham Hall from car park*

1. From the car park, head west along the road in front of the Hall. Follow the road round to the left, then cross the grass following the bank of the lake as it bends to the right, past some fine London Plane trees, and around the head of the lake.

2. At the end of the lake turn right on to the track, then through a gate and proceed north, past a sycamore tree along a grassy track, across the field towards the church. There may well be sheep grazing in the field, and you may also see some of the many deer which have inhabited the park since the 1850s. The herd of fallow deer includes some 470 does and 137 bucks, which produce approximately 300-320 fawns from June onwards. A few red deer were integrated into the herd in 2006.

3. After a while you will reach St Withburga's church. The mound on which St Withburga sits is possibly an Iron Age burial site or a temple. It is composed of sand, probably left by the Ice Age glacier, 12 000 years ago. This substantial

*The famous agricultural pioneer, "Coke of Norfolk" followed a couple of generations after the Hall was built. He revolutionised British farming by introducing new strains of crops, improving animal husbandry, manuring the soil and pioneering fodder crops.*

*Hall and Lake*

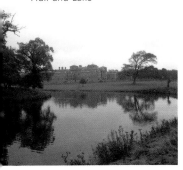

church, owned by the estate, has a medieval core, but was extensively rebuilt in the late 1860s, with a light airy interior, and a fine tiled floor. By all means climb the mound and visit the church, but leave the churchyard by the south gate (through which you entered) in order to continue the walk. Take the path almost opposite the churchyard gate, heading north-east past a yellow marker post until you reach a track.

 Turn right on to this track to head east, travelling parallel to the main road. You have now travelled just over a mile. This will bring you to the northern end of the lake, with fine views over the water. The lake was built about the same time as the Hall, by constructing a large curved dam across the creek

St Withburga's church

*The lake from the north*

*Fallow deer*

which took the water to the sea. The northern tip of what became the lake crossed what was then the coast road (almost 300 years ago!), which was diverted to the north to allow the lake to follow its designed shape. Go through the gate, and follow the path to the left of the lake, alongside the dam.

**5** Continue to follow the lakeside path, ignoring all other paths, as it eventually bends round to head south.

**6** After a while, take the left turn in the woods, past the red and yellow post, to head towards the Monument. This was built to commemorate the achievements of "Coke of Norfolk", many of which are depicted on the panels or by the figures on the column. It was erected after his death in 1842 and paid for by public subscription.

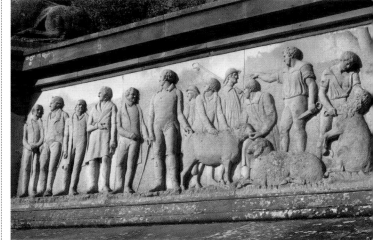

*Monument detail*

**7** Then, unless you particularly wish to return to the lakeside, head due south across the grass directly back towards the Hall, enjoying the magnificent views of the Hall as you proceed. A visit to the Hall and/or the adjacent "Bygones" museum is well worth while, or at least sample the excellent home-made ice cream on sale at the café, before returning to your car.

*The Monument*

# 3 **Stiffkey**

**Home Hill:** *a grassy hill and an infamous vicar*

This short walk takes you through a dairy farm, and up a steep grassy hill, returning through a small wood, and along the edge of fields. Shorts are not recommended for this walk, as you will encounter several nettles! In 1932 the infamous "Rector of Stiffkey", Harold Davidson, was found guilty of "systematic misbehaviour" with "poor unfortunate girls" in London. The verdict made world wide news, and poor de-frocked Harold finished his years preaching from a lions' cage in Skegness. He was fatally attacked by "Freddie" the lion in 1938, and his surviving relatives are still campaigning to prove his innocence.

**Difficulty:** 🥾 🥾 🥾
**Start/Parking:** Roadside, just south of the bridge on the Binham Road (about 100 yards south of its junction with the main coast road)
**Map Ref:** TF 971430
Nearest postcode NR23 1QP
**Distance:** 1.1 miles
**Nearest toilets:** Red Lion Pub (for customers only)
**Refreshments:** Red Lion pub or shop in village
**Terrain:** Steep grassy hill. Woodland. Grassy paths
**Transport:** Coasthopper bus
**Pushchairs:** No

*Map labels:* A149 · River · Stiffkey · Damson Lane · Home Hill · Cowshed · Binham Road · Gate · 1 · 2 · 3 · 4

500 m

*Home Hill*

①  Head west along the public bridleway close to where you have parked, through a gateway, and along a concrete track past a cowshed, which usually has some residents! Right near the bridge where you parked there used to be a small watermill, but this fell into disuse in 1881, and only a few bricks remain to show where it once stood. Continue west over a stile at the end of the track, keeping a watch out for cattle that may be grazing.

*In medieval times, Stiffkey was a coastal port, but longshore drift has left the village about a mile from the sea now!*

②  Continue along the left edge of a meadow, then soon go left over another stile and start climbing the hill. Go to the right of the gorse bush, then continue your direction down a little, then on to the top of the next hill, admiring the views of the surrounding countryside from the top. Continue towards the trees, and head for a gate and stile at the left-hand edge of the trees.

③  Go over the stile, and continue along the path through the

*Woodland path*

retrace your steps past the cowshed back to your car.

trees, still heading west, taking care to avoid the nettles! At the waymark, follow the path to the right through the nettles into the trees. You will have covered about half a mile. The path heads downhill quite steeply to the gate at the bottom. Go over the stile, then keep to the right side of the field down to the next gate.

**4** Climb over the stile here then turn right to head north-east along the path. Keep to the raised path, known as Damson Lane, along the right edge of the field, following the hedge as it curves round, to eventually reach yet another stile. Go over this stile and continue heading east to the final stile, then

*Autumn colours*

*The Red Lion*

# 4 **Blakeney**

***Kettlehill and Quay:*** *by open marshes, farmland and little boats*

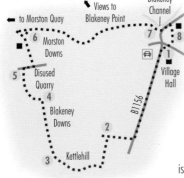

A pleasant walk across farmland with views across Blakeney harbour towards Blakeney Point, returning across the marshes and along the quayside. During the last few hundred years, the process of longshore drift has created a 4-mile long spit of sand and shingle to the north of the village, known as Blakeney Point. The River Glaven, now silted up to the extent that it is only knee deep at low tide, diverts around the Point, and the village is now a mile from the sea, with mudflats in between. The Point is still growing as the power of the sea continues to reshape the coastline.

**Difficulty:** 🥾 🥾
**Start/Parking:** Blakeney Village hall, just off A149 coast road, opposite turning to quay
**Map Ref:** TG 026438
Nearest postcode NR25 7PF
**Distance:** 2.5 miles
**Nearest toilets:** Wiveton Bell (0.8 miles - customers only)
**Refreshments:** Blakeney Quay – Teas and ice creams. Toilets at Blakeney Quay
**Terrain:** Farmland paths and the coast path
**Transport:** Coasthopper bus
**Pushchairs:** With difficultty

**1** Leave the car park by the main entrance, and turn left on to the road. This is the B1156. Walk along this for 0.36 miles heading South, until you get to a public foot-path sign. Turn right here to head west along a surfaced drive, with fine views of the coast to your right.

*Path to Kettle Hill*

**2** After a further 0.16 miles, you reach a waymark, where you turn left into a field. Follow the path along the right edge of this field, which will bend to the right shortly to head west. This is Kettlehill Plantation, and Blakeney Church will be visible at times behind you.

**3** Eventually you will turn right to go through the trees, then turn left to follow the left edge of another field. You will get occasional views of the sea. Soon your path bends to the right to continue round the left edge of the field, and you will be heading north. When you reach the corner of the field, there will be a large thatched house on the hill towering over you.

**4** Turn left through the gap in the hedge, and keep to the right edge of another field, as the path gently curves to the right. The area to your right is a disused quarry, Morston Church can be seen to your left, and ahead the sailing boats in Blakeney Channel. When you reach the road you will have covered 1.2 miles, and this is the half-way point.

**5** Go through the gate turning right for a few yards along

*House on the Hill*

*Path to the marsh*

the busy road (the A149 Coast Road), then cross the road and turn left at the Public Footpath sign to head North again. The grassy path takes you past a flint cottage then down a gentle slope to the marshes. At the bottom, you could turn left and head towards Morston Quay (you are roughly halfway there from Blakeney), which is a splendid walk, but you would need to retrace your steps to return.

(6) Instead, turn right on to the path which heads East towards Blakeney Quay. You will have fields on your right, and Blakeney Marshes, with views towards Blakeney

*Village sign*

*Blakeney Boats*

Point on your left. You have covered 1.5 miles. Keep to this path for a while until you cross a small grassy area, which takes you on to Blakeney Quay, close to the village sign.

**7** Keep close to the water's edge as you continue east for a short distance until you reach Blakeney Hotel. You have the option of proceeding a little further to get a cup of tea or ice cream, (or find toilets) but you need to return to this point. In the Middle Ages Blakeney was one of the top 10 British harbours. In 1347, the port provided ships for King Edward III's siege of Calais at the start of the Hundred Years War, and two hundred years later, when the Spanish Armada threatened invasion, Blakeney, Cley and Wiveton mustered an impressive 36 ships for the navy. Blakeney was one of the few ports allowed to trade in silver, gold and horses, while other imports included coal from Newcastle and stone quarried in Northamptonshire. Exports included locally grown wheat and wool.

( 8 ) Head South up the drive beside the hotel, with the hotel on your left and holiday accommodation on your right. The

*Blakeney harbour was first used, it is believed, by the Vikings, more than 1000 years ago, when the River Glaven was navigable from the sea.*

*Blakeney Harbour*

drive curves to the right at the top, then crosses The Pastures to get to the main road, passing the Millennium Stone on your left. Cross the road, turn right towards the bus shelter, left through the gap in the hedge, and you are back in your car park.

*The Juno*

*The Pastures*

# 5 Holt

***Town and Spout Hills:*** *excellent shops, art galleries, meadows and an old railway line*

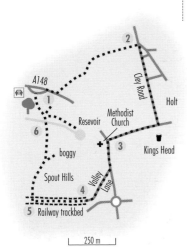

Holt has an excellent choice of contemporary and traditional art galleries, cafes, antique, gift and fine food shops; all contained in a maze of streets, alleyways and courtyards fanning out from the main High Street, and all within easy walking distance of each other. This short walk of just over a mile takes you through the town centre, along a short stretch of old railway trackbed, returning to the start across meadows, crossing a stream which used to flow from Holt's water supply.

**Difficulty:**
**Start/Parking:** Lay-by on Letheringsett Hill on left of A148 between Holt and Letheringsett
**Map Ref:** TG 073388
Nearest postcode NR25 6RY
**Distance:** 1.2 miles
**Refreshments:** Holt Town Centre
**Toilets:** Holt Town Centre
**Terrain:** Easy climbs, some steps, pavements, good paths
**Transport:** Various buses (see www.carlberry.co.uk). North Norfolk Railway 1 mile away
**Pushchairs:** With difficulty

**1** Cross the main road and head along the pavement up the hill towards the town. Very soon, take a footpath left to head north-west up a steeper hill with a few shallow steps which soon bend to the right. At the top, go up a few steps on to a residential road. Turn left, then continue your direction through the small housing estate on to the Cley Road.

**2** Turn right to head south along Cley Road into the town centre. By all means pause in the town to enjoy the delightful shops and cafes of Holt, but to continue the walk turn right at the Kings Head, towards the Methodist Church.

**3** Turn left at the busy junction into the Norwich Road. You

*Pereers Wood*

have now covered half a mile. Get to the right hand side of the road, using the crossing if necessary, and continue heading south along the right hand side of the road, until you turn right at the school into Valley Lane. When the road runs out, continue along the track, ignoring the path to the left,

then follow the track to the right past a meadow, where there are usually some horses.

**4** You will now be on the trackbed of the old M&GN railway from Holt to Melton Constable. The Midland and Great

*Methodist Church*

Northern Joint Railway (known locally as the "Muddle and Go Nowhere") used to run through from the Midlands to Cromer via Kings Lynn, Fakenham, Melton Constable and Holt. The use of this line declined as road traffic became more popular from the 1930s onwards, and most of the line closed in February 1959, although the most easterly section, from Melton Constable to Cromer, including the section covered in this walk, enjoyed a reprieve. In April

*Old Chapel, Cley Road*

*Old trackbed of the Midland & Great Northern Railway*

1964, however, Dr Beeching closed most of this, leaving just the three miles from Sheringham to Cromer, which still exists as part of the Sheringham to Norwich "Bittern Line". Continue along the trackbed for a while, then into the trees, imagining the steam trains thundering along what is now a tranquil woodland path.

**5** Turn right up a flight of steps, and follow the path on to grassy heathland. This area is Spout

*Spout Hills*

*Holt existed as a town before the Norman invasion and is recorded in the Doomsday Book of 1086. However, a great fire destroyed much of the town in 1708 and Holt was therefore rebuilt in the Georgian style of that time.*

Hills, which can be muddy in places, so stick to the main paths as you head gently downhill, and you should soon spot the valley ahead. Keep to the main path, as any deviations to the right can be boggy, and continue down to the stream. This stream flows down from the remains of a small disused reservoir to your right, which used to supply the town of Holt with water. You have now covered 1 mile.

**6** After crossing the stream, you have a choice: You can take the right hand path to visit the old reservoir, you can go straight ahead up a slope to a grassy area where children can play, or you can bear slightly left to take the path through the bushes back towards the layby where you parked. Whichever option you take, you will need to make your way back to this path in order to get to the 5-bar gate which leads to the lay-by.

*Stream*

*The Old Reservoir*

# 6 Salthouse

***Walsey Hills and beach:*** *beautiful shingle shore, marsh and fields*

A wonderful walk taking in another section of the Norfolk coast path, and also the fields which cross Walsey Hills. The walk starts from the old Post Office in the village of Salthouse, which only closed in 2007 when the postmistress retired. Walsey Hill is home to a Norfolk Ornithologists Association (NOA) reserve, and the path takes you close to one of their bird hides. You will also see Norfolk reeds growing on Snipes Marsh. This is reputed to be the finest thatching material in the world, but the quantities growing here are not commercially viable. The Dun Cow pub or the renowned Cookies Crab Shop will provide you with food and drink, with al fresco facilities if you wish, but both establishments get extremely busy in the season.

*Map:*

North Sea

6

Arnolds Marsh

7

8

Optional Short Cut

Flood Siren ■

Walsey Hills

5

The Dun Cow

Salthouse Marshes

1

Snipes Marsh

4

3

Views to sea

2

9

■ 🚗

Hedges

Sarbury Hill

✚ Salthouse Church

| 1000 m |

**Difficulty:** 💚 💚
**Start/Parking:** At Salthouse outside the old Post Office on A149 Coast Road
**Map Ref:** TG 075439
Nearest postcode NR25 7AJ
**Distance:** 3.3 miles
**Refreshments:** Salthouse Dun Cow pub, Cookies Crab Shop, ice creams from the roadside
**Toilets:** Salthouse Dun Cow pub (for customers)
**Terrain:** Fields, good paths, and a shingle bank. One short, steep descent, otherwise gentle gradients or flat walking
**Transport:** Coasthopper bus
**Pushchairs:** No

*Path across field*

1. From the red phone box near your car, cross the road to head due west along a narrow path labelled "public footpath". Climb a stile into a meadow, and walk along the right edge of this meadow to get to another stile which takes you into a field. You will now be enjoying fine sea views over the marshes to your right. Continue heading west by crossing this field, soon following a hedgerow.

*The Old Post Office*

2. At the end of this field, the path goes into the blackberry bushes. Follow the path between the bushes, which will soon fall quite sharply, and then fork left when the path splits (right would simply take you to the main coast road). Your path will take you through a hedge into another field, which you cross, still keeping your westerly direction. Go through a gap in the hedge, and continue your direction following the left edge of the next field. At the end of the hedgerow, continue heading west across the open field, gently falling towards the hedge in front of you.

3. When you reach the hedge, you have the option of turning right, and following the hedgerow back to the main road, and thence back to the village. However, to follow the recommended walk, continue your direction for a few more yards, following the path down to the T-junction at the bottom.

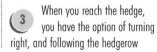

*Many types of bird can be spotted in Arnolds Marsh; Roseate terns were seen here in 2007.*

**4** Turn right into the tunnel of hedges, and continue past the NOA observatory to the main coast road (A149). Turn Left here, with Snipes Marsh on your left, but soon cross the road to head towards the "public footpath" sign on your right, and turn right here. You will now have covered 1 mile.

**5** Head due north along the path on top of the bank heading towards the sea. At the end, after about half a mile, you will go past some water on your right. This area is Arnolds Marsh.

**6** Climb the shingle bank on to the coast path. The village of Cley lies to the south-west, but you will turn right to head east, back

*Tunnel of hedges*

towards Salthouse. Walking along this bank can be quite exhilarating, with the sea on your left, and the marshes to your right, although much of the bank has now been

flattened by the sea, and it is no longer being re-built each time this happens, thanks to the Government's controversial policy of "Managed Retreat".

**7** After about ¾ mile you will have the option of turning right to follow a path between two ditches back to the main road, and thence back to the village, but I recommend that you continue along the bank for a further third of a mile until you reach a small grassy hill on your right. You will spot the village flood siren on a pole in the marshes as you go past.

**8** When you reach the grassy hill (which is pretty well in line with Salthouse Church) turn right to head for the concrete wartime look-out, known as "Little Eye", but before reaching it turn right along a grassy path heading south towards the village alongside a wire fence. Your grassy path will take you past a patch of water or mud, then over a small wooden bridge with a waymark, and back to the village with the tower of Salthouse Church straight ahead of you, and usually cattle in the fields either side. Salthouse church was completed in 1503, but building of the tower might have started up to 250 years earlier. It is a magnificent church building which houses an annual not-to-be-missed contemporary arts festival.

**9** At the main road, cross the road, then turn right, and return to your car, taking well earned refreshment at the Dun Cow or Cookies Crab Shop.

*Beach, towards Sheringham*

*The Dun Cow*

# 7 Kelling

**Heath and Holgate Hill:** *heathland paths and fine sea views*

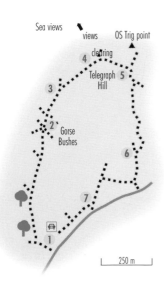

A short walk over heathland, with some fine views over the sea. The walk can be shortened by cutting across the heath at any point to head back toward the car park. Watch out for the gorse if you are wearing sandals or shorts! About 12 000 years ago, an advancing ice sheet ground to a halt more or less where Kelling Heath and its neighbour Salthouse heath now stand. As climate warmed at the end of the Ice Age, the ice melted, depositing millions of tons of sand, gravel and larger stones, and forming what we now call the Holt-Cromer Ridge. Vegetation returned and eventually trees appeared, although browsing animals such as rodents, deer, wild cattle and horses gradually reduced the vegetation to the heathland we now enjoy.

**Difficulty:**
**Start/Parking:** Car park just off the road from Weybourne to Holt, on the right as you head for Holt. Look for the turning where the road dips
**Map Ref:** TG 099417
Nearest postcode NR25 7ER
**Distance:** 1.5 miles
**Refreshments:** EMCY Garden Centre, across the road, towards Holt
**Toilets:** EMCY Garden Centre (for customers)
**Terrain:** Level heathland paths
**Transport:** No
**Pushchairs:** With difficulty

*Silver birch trees*

1 Walk back down the slope towards the car park entrance, but turn right into a small grassy path (with nettles) before you reach the road. Follow this path for about 10 yards, then the path forks right (the left hand path goes nowhere!), and follow the path across the heath, past silver birch trees. You may be able to make out the boundary between the heath and the adjoining field on your left. Continue heading north along this path, ignoring forks and turnings to the left (which will take you down to the coast road at Kelling).

2 Eventually you will reach a clump of tall gorse bushes, about 10 feet (3 metres) high, where several paths meet. Go right then immediately left to continue your direction through the bushes, and after a few yards there will be another meeting of paths. Take the path that is effectively 2nd left, ignoring the 1st left which heads downhill. This will take you between some gorse bushes and on to a stony path, which starts to get wider.

3 Keep to the main path, and after a short while take the right hand fork to keep to the level stony path, still heading north. There

*Gorse*

is much heather about, and you may soon get glimpses of the sea to your left through the gorse as the ground falls away to the north. After a while, the heath to your right will become much flatter, with caravans possibly visible in the distance.

**(4)** You will reach a clearing where several paths meet, with fine sea views to your left. You are standing on Telegraph Hill, and have travelled 0.75 miles

If you wish, deviate to your left to admire the view. The houses of Weynor Gardens will be below you, with Muckleborough Hill in the distance. The Pheasant Hotel is also below you to your left. Return to the main path, which you follow as it curves right, still keeping the sea to your left.

**(5)** As a diversion, you can take a narrow path to the left when

*The Heath*

you are on the cusp of the curve. This will take you through the gorse into some bushes where the old Ordnance Survey triangulation pillar can be found, the surrounding vegetation would need to be cut back for this one to be much use now! Retrace your steps back to the path to continue the walk. You will see more caravans in the distance ahead. Keep to the right hand path when the main paths fork, and after a short while you will have fine views of Skelding Hill in the distance on your left. You will now be

*Satellite technology has now rendered Ordnance Survey triangulation pillars redundant for map-making*

OS triangulation point

*View east from Telegraph Hill*

heading South, and there is lots of gorse! The path gets more narrow in places, but eventually you will emerge on to a wider path which goes left to the road. You have covered 1.2 miles.

**6** Where the paths meet, ignore the path to the road, but turn right and follow a track which heads north-west, and head across the heath. After a short while, fork left then left again on to a wide path to head south-west.

**7** Just before you reach the road again, turn right on to a narrow path running parallel to the road. This will take you across the heath, ignoring a path to the right, then across a gravel area back to the car park.

*Dusk on the heath*

# 8 Sheringham

***Beeston Hump:*** *exploring the town, an open common and glacial moraine*

This walk takes you over Beeston Hump, with fabulous coast views. The town of Sheringham started off in medieval times in what is now Upper Sheringham, a mile inland. A fishing community subsequently became established by the sea, but the town's reputation as a holiday resort really started when the railways arrived in the late 19th century, when the town grew rapidly. The hills surrounding Sheringham date back much further, however, comprising of debris or "moraine" dumped by the glacier which just reached the tip of North Norfolk during the last Ice Age. As the ice melted, the hills we now call Morley hill, Skelding Hill, Beeston Hump, were left. This walk takes you up the last of these.

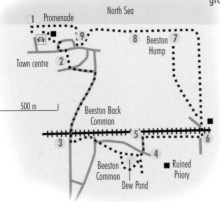

**Difficulty:** 🐾 🐾 🐾 🐾
**Start/Parking:** Cliff Road car park, just east of Sheringham town centre. (Council Charges)
**Map Ref:** TG 161435
Nearest postcode NR26 8BW
**Distance:** 2.0 miles (2.2 including the priory)
**Refreshments:** Sheringham town centre and East Promenade
**Toilets:** Sheringham East Promenade (in summer). Otherwise in town centre
**Terrain:** Roads and clear paths, with a steep grassy hill
**Transport:** Sanders and First Easter buses. Bittern Line and Poppy Line Railways
**Pushchairs:** No

① From the car park head east along a small path behind the gardens of a row of cliff-top terraced houses, then turn right past a row of lock-up garages, then left to get to Vincent Road. Turn right along Vincent Road, then left into Cliff Road. Head up the road until it starts to bend left, when you should turn right into a narrow track between the houses.

② At the end of this track, turn left into the Avenue, then fork right at the phone box into Avenue South, past Bees Hall, which is home to local artist Brian Lewis. At the end of this road, turn right into Curtis Lane, and head south down this road to get to Beeston Back Common, continuing south along the road

*East Promenade*

through the common to the railway bridge.

③ Turn left into a path immediately after the bridge. Proceed past a derelict farmhouse, and continue along the northern edge of the common, with houses to your left. If the path is not too muddy, take the grassy path to the right of the stream

to the Dew Pond, then turn left at the T junction and over a small concrete bridge back to the road. The Dew Pond is filled naturally by ground water, or even dew, but not fed by a stream. This ancient pond was restored by volunteers in 2007, and the following year was found to host a "Mudwort", a plant not seen in Norfolk since 1914.

*The Dew Pond*

**4** When the tarmac road gives way to a track, you have the option of continuing for a short distance to view Beeston Priory on your right. The ruins are a "World Heritage Site" and are in the care of English Heritage and North Norfolk District Council. After leaving the priory you need to return to the tarmac road, and then head north into Church Lane, until you reach the railway line. This track is the main line to Cromer, and then Norwich, known as the "Bittern Line".

**5** Turn right to follow a narrow path east alongside the railway. This takes you past a meadow

*Beeston Regis Augustinian Priory was founded in 1216 from one of the 2 churches in the parish (the other being All Saints Beeston Regis, still in use). The Priory existed until 1538 when King Henry VIII banned the Catholic religion and ordered the dissolution of the Monasteries and Priories. The remaining ruins include a 75 foot nave with a chancel and 2 later chapels.*

where horses are often found grazing to your right, and then past some allotments, where the track widens.

**6** At the old crossing keeper's cottage, turn left to cross the railway by the gated crossing. Take care, as trains regularly use this line. Continue along one of the two grassy paths ahead, in a broadly northerly direction towards the sea, with the caravan site to your right, until you

*Farmhouse*

*The Bittern Line*

reach the North Norfolk Coastal Path on the cliff. You will have covered about 1.2 miles

7 When you reach the cliff top, turn left to head west towards Beeston Hump (or Bump, as many call it). When you reach the corner of the field at the foot of the Hump you have a choice. Either fork left to go around the base of the hill, or straight on to climb the Hump. If you can

make it I would recommend the latter, as the views are well worth it.

At the top there are seats, a disused Ordnance Survey triangulation point, and stunning views of the sea, Sheringham, and surrounding countryside. To the west, you may be able to see as far as Blakeney Point on a clear day. To the east, Cromer lighthouse should clearly be visible. The mast to the south-east is the local television booster at Roman Camp.

*Beeston Hump*

*Sheringham from the Hump under light snow*

(8) Continue down the hill heading west, following the path, with the sea to your right. The path continues downhill past a putting green and on to a road.

(9) Turn right down a concrete slope flanked by grassy banks, then down a flight of blue brick steps down to the promenade. Turn left to head west along the promenade to the large shelter (which is also a waste water pumping station), then left after the cafe, up a flight of steps to Cliff Road car park.

*Beeston Priory ruins*

# 9 East Runton

### Roman Camp and Congham Hill:
*through woodland and along country paths*

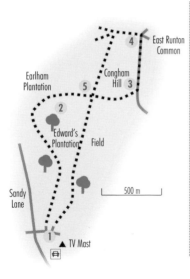

This walk starts on the Holt-Cromer Ridge at "Roman Camp", arguably the highest point of Norfolk, about 100m above sea level, and heads downhill through the woodlands of Edwards Plantation and Earlham Plantation before heading east towards East Runton Common, returning around Congham Hill and back uphill through the woods. The name Roman Camp is probably misleading, as there is no evidence of Roman occupation here! At the top of the hill is a 46m transmission mast, a relay for the 4 main TV channels plus local and digital radio from the Tacolneston transmitter in South Norfolk.

**Difficulty:** 🥾 🥾 🥾
**Start/Parking:** Parking area just off the road at Roman Camp, with post box and NT sign. Close to TV mast
**Map Ref:** TG 186413
Nearest postcode NR27 9NE
**Distance:** 1.8 miles
**Refreshments:** Roman Camp Public House (half mile away)
**Toilets:** Roman Camp Public House (for customers)
**Terrain:** Woodland and countryside paths with a long descent and climb
**Transport:** Railway – Bittern Line – West Runton Station (1 mile)
**Pushchairs:** With difficulty – some kissing gates and a bumpy climb

1 From the parking area, head away from the road, and turn left to take the track way, marked with an acorn, down the hill through the trees. This is a section of the North Norfolk Coast path, and has a good solid stony surface. Continue heading north for some time, then the path will bend to the right, and you will reach the entrance to the Camping Club site.

2 Keep heading east along the path, which now becomes narrower, and the countryside more open. You will soon reach a cross-roads, and you should continue your direction along the sometimes muddy coast path, heading east, past Congham Hill on your left. Continue gently downhill through two kissing

West Runton transmission mast

*Barn with owl or bat-holes*

gates and across a stream. Then you cross a boggy meadow and soon reach a track. To continue heading east would take you eventually to Cromer, but turn left here, along the track, now heading north.

**3** The track, called Banville Lane, soon becomes surfaced, and brings you out at the edge of East Runton Common. You have now covered a mile, and are more than half way through the walk. This is a lovely common, flanking the lane heading inland from the coast road for about half a mile. Further north the lane will go under two very fine late 19th century railway viaducts, but this route does not take you that far. The two ponds on the common are home to many dozens of friendly ducks and geese who would be happy to meet you if you wish to explore the common.

**4** If you do, you will need to return to this point and turn

left at the "Public Bridleway" sign to head west, under the trees. Shortly, when the paths fork, keep to the left-hand path and head for the TV mast in the distance. Follow this path for a while, gently climbing and heading

*Path towards TV mast*

*Excavations have shown Beacon Hill to have been an iron-working settlement in Saxon and medieval times, which may well have had Roman origins.*

south-west, and you will reach the cross-roads that you met on your outward journey.

(5) Cross over, and continue to head south-west towards the TV mast. Go through the kissing gate and take a clear path across the field, where there is obvious evidence of grazing cattle. Go through yet another kissing gate into the woods, and fol-low the woodland path, still heading south-west, which will now climb the

hill back to the parking area. Some of the "trees" you will walk under are actually overgrown rhododendron

bushes! This path becomes a bit steeper than the one you walked down at the start of the walk, but is more direct, and you will soon reach the top. Blame the last Ice Age for the steepness of the climb, as the huge glacier bulldozed all this material (mainly sand and stones) as it headed south, then stopped after it had just clipped what is now the north Norfolk coast! The glacier melted about 12 000 years ago (global warming?) leaving the hills you are now climbing.

When you return to the parking area, you may wish to take a look at the TV mast before returning to your car.

*View along the return path*

*Congham Hill*

## 10 Overstrand

### Newmans Hill and golf course:
exhilarating clifftop walk and fine sea views

This walk starts in the "Millionaire's Village" of Overstrand and heads inland to climb on to higher land close to the old railway line, with fine views over the sea. After a short unavoidable stretch along the main road, you climb to Cromer lighthouse, where the views are magnificent, and you return along the stunning clifftops.

This is Clement Scott's Poppyland at its finest, although you are unlikely to see poppies along this stretch as it is occupied by the Royal Cromer Golf Club. Gorse abounds however, releasing its heady scent should you be walking in the summer months.

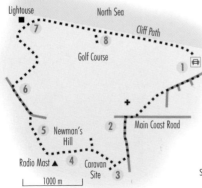

**Difficulty:** 🥾 🥾
**Start/Parking:** Overstrand - Sea front car park (North Norfolk District Council charge)
**Map Ref:** TG 247411
Nearest postcode NR27 0PF
**Distance:** 2.8 miles
**Refreshments:** Overstrand — Cliff Top Cafe (just to east of car park)
**Toilets:** Public toilets in car park
**Terrain:** Woodland paths, pavements and cliff tops
**Transport:** Sanders coach services from Cromer
**Pushchairs:** With difficulty — some mud and gradients

From the car park head west along the road leading away from the sea, and continue until the road bends sharp left, when you should continue your direction along a straight narrow path. This path eventually emerges on to the main coast road (B1159), and here you turn right to walk along the main road past St Martin's church.

Soon turn left to head inland along Northrepps Road. You will soon pass an old railway embankment on your right (the one on the left has been demolished to make way for houses). Continue south along the road a little further, then turn right through a gate into a grassy area, and take the uphill path to your right.

*Lutyens chapel*

Keep to this wide path through the trees as you pass by a caravan site. After a while the path bends to the left with an optional right fork. The right fork would take you to the railway trackbed, which you could follow through the cutting towards Cromer, but the views are limited, and the path can be muddy. You should, instead, follow the main path as it bends left and climbs uphill. Continue heading west as you

pass the caravans to your left. The path will bend right then left and lead you to a grassy area with goalposts and a radio mast.

Leave the path and cross the grass towards the mast, enjoying the sea views to the north as you do so — you may just see Cromer lighthouse. This is Newmans Hill, and

*Overstrand Cliff*

you have travelled about a mile. Continue heading west, past the seat, and take the path into the trees beyond the mast. Keep to the main path as it bends right round to the right and starts heading quite sharply downhill. There will be an old wartime pillbox in the bushes to your right should you care to climb up to it and investigate.

*St Martin's Church*

 You will soon reach the remains of an old railway bridge, and you should cross the trackbed at this point, and follow the path to the left of the bridge as it climbs and bends to the left. The trackbed is that of the old Midland and Great Northern railway which ran from Cromer to Mundesley along the coast, then inland to North Walsham. The

Cromer to Mundesley section closed as early as April 1952, although it would have been a scenic route in its day. The path emerges on the coast road, and you will need to cross this road and follow it west, ie towards Cromer, past the 30mph sign, the Sea Scout HQ and the small Catholic church, until you reach Cromer Golf Club.

Turn right here, to follow the public footpath to the right of the fence up the hill north towards the sea. Stay on the track right to the top and you will emerge at Cromer lighthouse. An earlier lighthouse was built following Charles II's restoration in 1660, which acquired a rotating oil light in 1792. The sea

*Newmans Hill*

admire the views of Cromer to your left, including the highest parish church tower in Norfolk, before returning to the path, and taking the clear path east between the gorse. Ignore the path to the left which would take you via "Happy Valley" into Cromer. Go past the seats, and continue to the cliff top, where you should turn right and head east towards Overstrand. You have now covered 1.7 miles. You will be walking along the edge of the Royal Cromer Golf Club along a path

encroached rapidly, with substantial cliff falls during the 19th century, and the building was finally destroyed by a landslip in 1866. The present lighthouse, 18m tall, was built in 1833, became electric-powered in 1958,

and converted to automatic operation in June 1990, now monitored from Harwich by Trinity House.

 Stroll across to the helipad, rarely used these days, and

*Before the erection of a lighthouse at Cromer, ships were guided by fires lit on the 50m tower of Cromer parish church.*

marked on the OS map as a public right of way. The golf course was established in the late 1880s, and has been enjoyed by queens, princes, dukes, earls, knights, barons, MP's, and other members of the landed gentry, as well as famous names like Sir Arthur Conan-Doyle and Oscar Wilde. Please keep away from the cliff edge, and beware of errant golf balls as you head east along the cliff top. The views are superb along this section of the walk, with the iconic Cromer Pier behind you, and the "golf ball" of Trimingham radar station in the distance ahead. Stay on the cliff path until eventually you will see the village of Overstrand in front of you.

(8) After a while you will reach the erect railway sleeper, and you should ignore the path to the right, which would take you to the main road, but marvel at the periscope presumably provided to help golfers to track their shots! At the end of the golf course, continue east along the cliff, past some houses and a small grassy field, and through some bushes to return to the car park.

*Royal Cromer golf course*

*Cromer lighthouse*